WELCOME TO THE U.S.A.

OHIO

Written by Ann Heinrichs   Illustrated by Matt Kania
Content Adviser: Erin Bartlett, Interpretive Programs Department,
Ohio Historical Society, Columbus, Ohio

The Child's World

Published in the United States of America by The Child's World®
PO Box 326 • Chanhassen, MN 55317-0326
800-599-READ • www.childsworld.com

Photo Credits
Cover: Wes Thompson/Corbis; frontispiece: Galen Rowell/Corbis.

Interior: Bob Evans Farm: 33; Center of Science and Industry – Toledo: 30; Corbis: 9 (Howie McCormick/Icon SMI), 17 (Joseph Sohm; ChromoSohm, Inc.), 21 (Owen Franken); Getty Images/AFP/Jeff Haynes: 34; The Goodyear Tire & Rubber Museum: 22; Honda: 26; National Museum of the US Air Force: 25; Ohio Caverns: 6; Picture Desk/Travelsite/Global: 13; Lee Snider/Photo Images/Corbis: 14, 18, 29; Wayne and Hoosier National Forests: 10.

Acknowledgments
The Child's World®: Mary Berendes, Publishing Director

Editorial Directions, Inc.: E. Russell Primm, Editorial Director; Katie Marsico, Associate Editor; Judith Shiffer, Assistant Editor; Matt Messbarger, Editorial Assistant; Susan Hindman, Copy Editor; Melissa McDaniel, Proofreader; Kevin Cunningham, Peter Garnham, Matt Messbarger, Olivia Nellums, Chris Simms, Molly Symmonds, Katherine Trickle, Carl Stephen Wender, Fact Checkers; Tim Griffin/IndexServ, Indexer; Cian Loughlin O'Day, Photo Researcher and Editor

The Design Lab: Kathleen Petelinsek, Design; Julia Goozen, Art Production

Library of Congress Cataloging-in-Publication Data
Heinrichs, Ann.
  Ohio / by Ann Heinrichs.
    p. cm. – (Welcome to the U.S.A.)
  Includes index.
  ISBN 1-59296-449-4 (library bound : alk. paper)
  1. Ohio—Juvenile literature. I. Title.
F491.3.H443 2006
977.1—dc22   2005000529

Ann Heinrichs is the author of more than 100 books for children and young adults. She has also enjoyed successful careers as a children's book editor and an advertising copywriter. Ann grew up in Fort Smith, Arkansas, and lives in Chicago, Illinois.

About the Author
Ann Heinrichs

Matt Kania loves maps and, as a kid, dreamed of making them. In school he studied geography and cartography, and today he makes maps for a living. Matt's favorite thing about drawing maps is learning about the places they represent. Many of the maps he has created can be found in books, magazines, videos, Web sites, and public places.

About the Map Illustrator
Matt Kania

On the cover: Do you like music? Be sure to check out the Rock 'n' Roll Hall of Fame.
On page one: The sun rises over the Cuyahoga River.

OUR OHIO TRIP

Ohio's Nickname:
The Buckeye State

WELCOME TO
OHIO

Ready for a grand tour of Ohio? You'll be glad you came! It's chock-full of things to discover.

You'll explore caves and creep through forests. You'll learn to milk cows and make candles. You'll ride a boat pulled by a horse. You'll learn how motorcycles are made. You'll see thousands of twins. And you'll watch rats playing basketball!

There's much more to explore, so buckle up. You can follow that loopy dotted line. Or else just skip around. Ohio, here we come!

As you travel through Ohio, watch for all the interesting facts along the way.

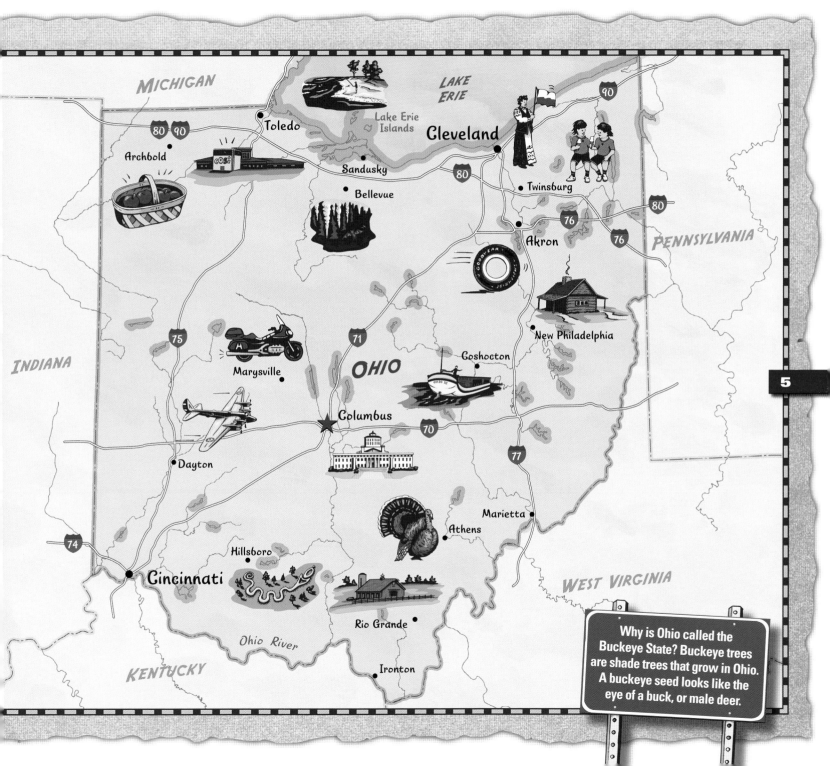

MICHIGAN

LAKE ERIE

Lake Erie Islands

Toledo

Archbold

GOSI

80 90

Cleveland

90

Sandusky

80

Twinsburg

80

Bellevue

76

PENNSYLVANIA

Akron

76

GOODYEAR

New Philadelphia

INDIANA

75

Marysville

OHIO

71

Coshocton

OHIO III

Columbus

70

Dayton

77

Marietta

Athens

Hillsboro

74

Cincinnati

Rio Grande

WEST VIRGINIA

Ohio River

Ironton

KENTUCKY

Why is Ohio called the Buckeye State? Buckeye trees are shade trees that grow in Ohio. A buckeye seed looks like the eye of a buck, or male deer.

Peter Rutan and Henry Homer discovered Seneca Caverns in 1872.

Grab your flashlight! It's time to explore Ohio Caverns in West Liberty.

Ohio's caves were formed by underground streams. The water wore away the rock, leaving tunnels.

Seneca Caverns in Bellevue

Peter and Henry were walking with their dog. The dog began chasing a rabbit. Both animals disappeared into a hole. Peter and Henry followed after them. Then *kerplunk*! The boys landed in a deep, underground cave. They had discovered Seneca **Caverns.** Now you can explore those caverns, too.

The Ohio River forms Ohio's southern border. Many other rivers flow south into the Ohio. Some rivers flow north into Lake Erie. This lake borders northern Ohio. Eastern Ohio is rugged and hilly. Rolling plains cover western Ohio. This region's rich soil makes great farmland.

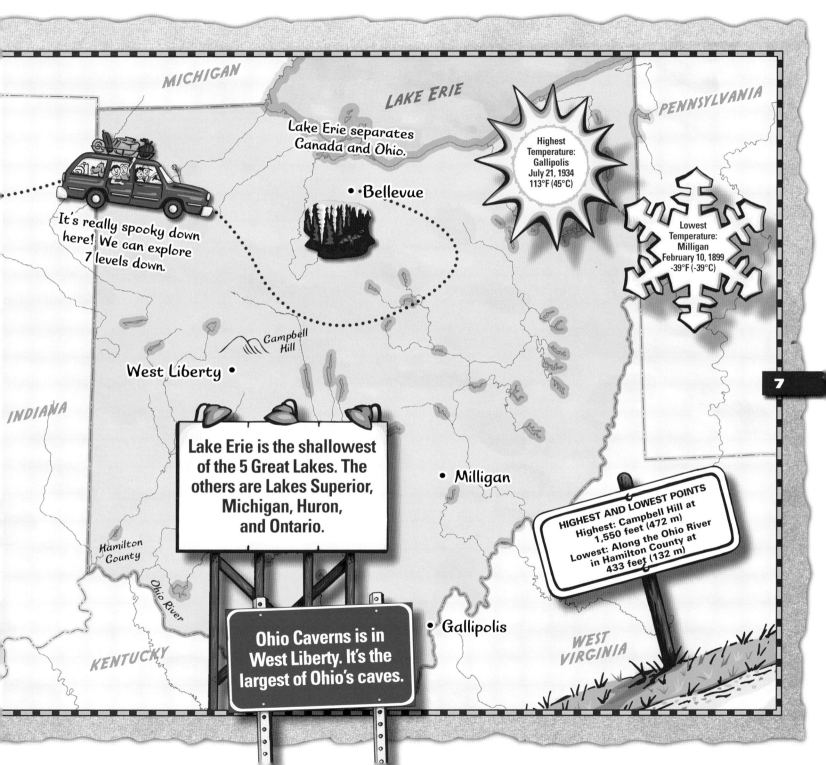

MICHIGAN

LAKE ERIE

PENNSYLVANIA

Lake Erie separates Canada and Ohio.

Highest Temperature: Gallipolis July 21, 1934 113°F (45°C)

Lowest Temperature: Milligan February 10, 1899 -39°F (-39°C)

• • Bellevue

It's really spooky down here! We can explore 7 levels down.

Campbell Hill

West Liberty •

INDIANA

Lake Erie is the shallowest of the 5 Great Lakes. The others are Lakes Superior, Michigan, Huron, and Ontario.

• Milligan

HIGHEST AND LOWEST POINTS
Highest: Campbell Hill at 1,550 feet (472 m)
Lowest: Along the Ohio River in Hamilton County at 433 feet (132 m)

Hamilton County

Ohio River

Ohio Caverns is in West Liberty. It's the largest of Ohio's caves.

• Gallipolis

WEST VIRGINIA

KENTUCKY

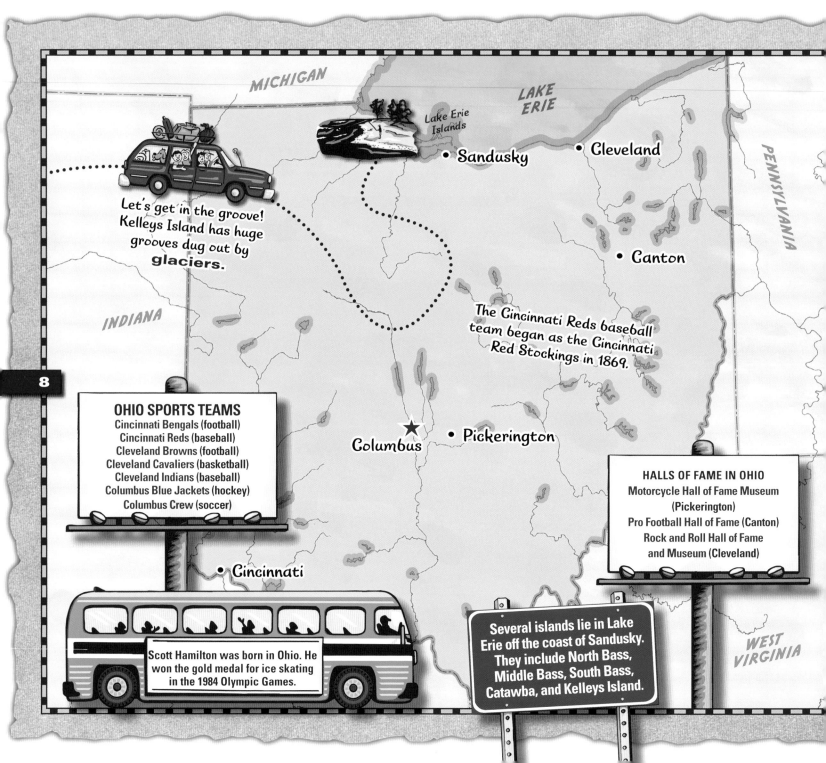

MICHIGAN

LAKE ERIE

Lake Erie Islands

• Sandusky

• Cleveland

PENNSYLVANIA

Let's get in the groove! Kelleys Island has huge grooves dug out by **glaciers.**

INDIANA

• Canton

The Cincinnati Reds baseball team began as the Cincinnati Red Stockings in 1869.

OHIO SPORTS TEAMS
Cincinnati Bengals (football)
Cincinnati Reds (baseball)
Cleveland Browns (football)
Cleveland Cavaliers (basketball)
Cleveland Indians (baseball)
Columbus Blue Jackets (hockey)
Columbus Crew (soccer)

★ Columbus

• Pickerington

HALLS OF FAME IN OHIO
Motorcycle Hall of Fame Museum
(Pickerington)
Pro Football Hall of Fame (Canton)
Rock and Roll Hall of Fame
and Museum (Cleveland)

• Cincinnati

Scott Hamilton was born in Ohio. He won the gold medal for ice skating in the 1984 Olympic Games.

Several islands lie in Lake Erie off the coast of Sandusky. They include North Bass, Middle Bass, South Bass, Catawba, and Kelleys Island.

WEST VIRGINIA

Fun on the Lake Erie Islands

Ohioans love to visit the Lake Erie islands. They go camping, hiking, and picnicking there. They can also go fishing, boating, and swimming. Some islands even have caves to explore. Ohio's eastern hills are great for hiking, too.

Some people enjoy watching team sports. Ohio sports fans have plenty to cheer about. Ohio is home to several sports teams. They play football, baseball, basketball, hockey, and soccer. College football fans are proud of the Buckeyes. They're the Ohio State University's champion football team.

Go, Buckeyes! Fans root for their favorite Ohio team.

9

The Ohio State Buckeyes won the National College Athletic Association (NCAA) football championship in 2002.

Watching Wildlife in Wayne National Forest

This baby owl calls Wayne National Forest home.

Walk softly, facing the wind. Then the animals won't hear or smell you. You'll see deer grazing on the forest floor. Wild turkeys strut through the leaves. Watch out! You might even see bobcats or bears.

River otters live near streams. They float on their backs in the water. If it's spring, you might spot ruffed grouse. They flutter and beat their wings. This makes a loud drumming sound. Males do this to attract a mate.

You're wandering through Wayne National Forest. It has three big sections. They're near Marietta, Athens, and Ironton. All three are great for watching animals!

River otters swim underwater to catch fish. On land, they may slide down a muddy slope on their bellies!

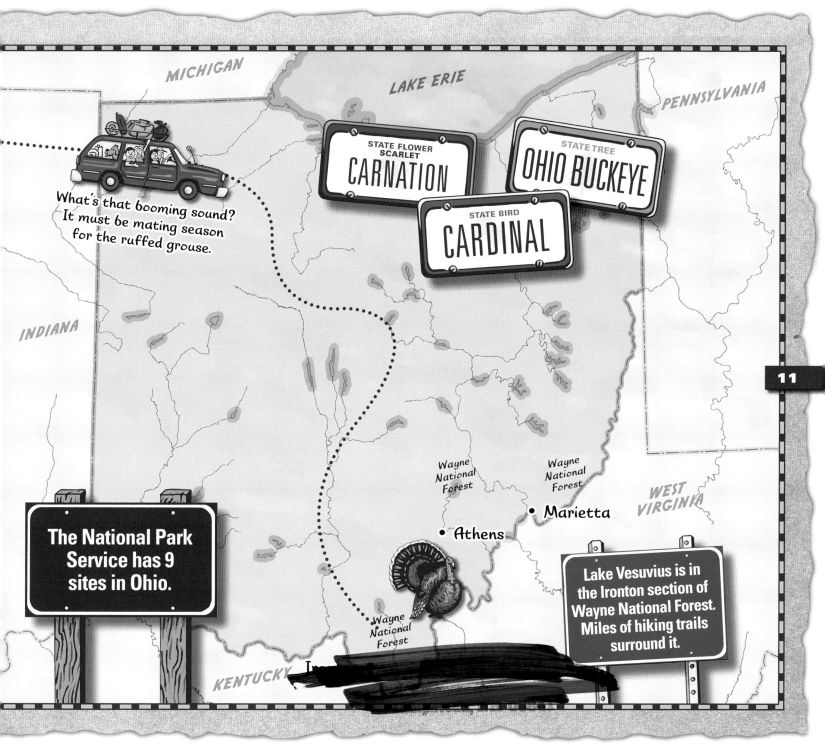

What's that booming sound? It must be mating season for the ruffed grouse.

STATE FLOWER
SCARLET
CARNATION

STATE TREE
OHIO BUCKEYE

STATE BIRD
CARDINAL

The National Park Service has 9 sites in Ohio.

Lake Vesuvius is in the Ironton section of Wayne National Forest. Miles of hiking trails surround it.

MICHIGAN

LAKE ERIE

PENNSYLVANIA

INDIANA

Wayne National Forest

Wayne National Forest

WEST VIRGINIA

• Marietta

• Athens

Wayne National Forest

KENTUCKY

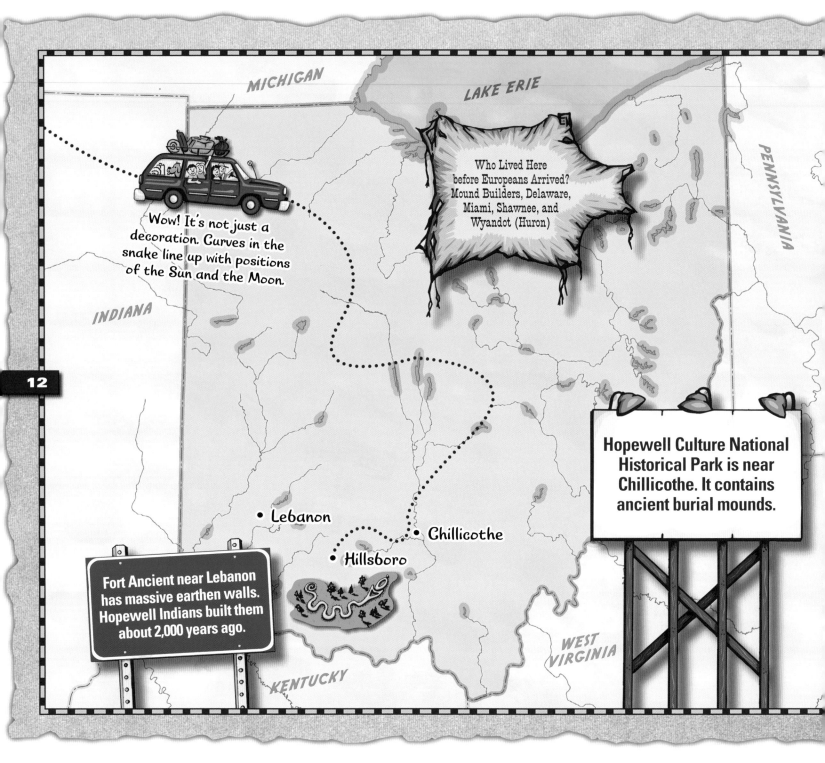

MICHIGAN

LAKE ERIE

PENNSYLVANIA

INDIANA

Wow! It's not just a decoration. Curves in the snake line up with positions of the Sun and the Moon.

Who Lived Here before Europeans Arrived? Mound Builders, Delaware, Miami, Shawnee, and Wyandot (Huron)

Hopewell Culture National Historical Park is near Chillicothe. It contains ancient burial mounds.

• Lebanon

• Chillicothe

• Hillsboro

Fort Ancient near Lebanon has massive earthen walls. Hopewell Indians built them about 2,000 years ago.

WEST VIRGINIA

KENTUCKY

The Great Serpent Mound near Hillsboro

The Great Serpent Mound winds through the forest. You can see it best from the air. It looks like a giant snake. Native Americans built it more than 1,000 years ago. They piled up soil to form the long mound. Ohio has many **prehistoric** Indian sites. People who lived there built huge **earthworks.** Later, several Indian groups lived in Ohio. They hunted in the forests and grew crops.

French explorers were the first Europeans in Ohio. They came from Canada, to the north. British **colonists** moved in from the Atlantic coast, too. France and Great Britain fought over North American lands. They made peace after Britain won in 1763.

Want to learn about Ohio's prehistoric Indians? Just visit the Great Serpent Mound!

Are you back in the 1700s? Nope! You're just touring Schoenbrunn Village.

The land that is now Ohio became part of the country's Northwest Territory in 1787.

Schoenbrunn Village near New Philadelphia

Log cabins look out over the cornfields. Crude log fences surround the land. A quiet, shady area is called God's Acre. It's a 200-year-old cemetery. You're visiting Schoenbrunn Village. **Missionaries** called Moravians settled there in 1772. They preached Christianity to the Delaware Indians.

The colonists soon fought Britain for their freedom. This fight was the Revolutionary War (1775–1783). The colonists won!

Settlers founded the town of Marietta in 1788. That was Ohio's first permanent white settlement. Indians were still fighting to keep their land. They lost the Battle of Fallen Timbers in 1794. Then they had to give up most of their Ohio lands.

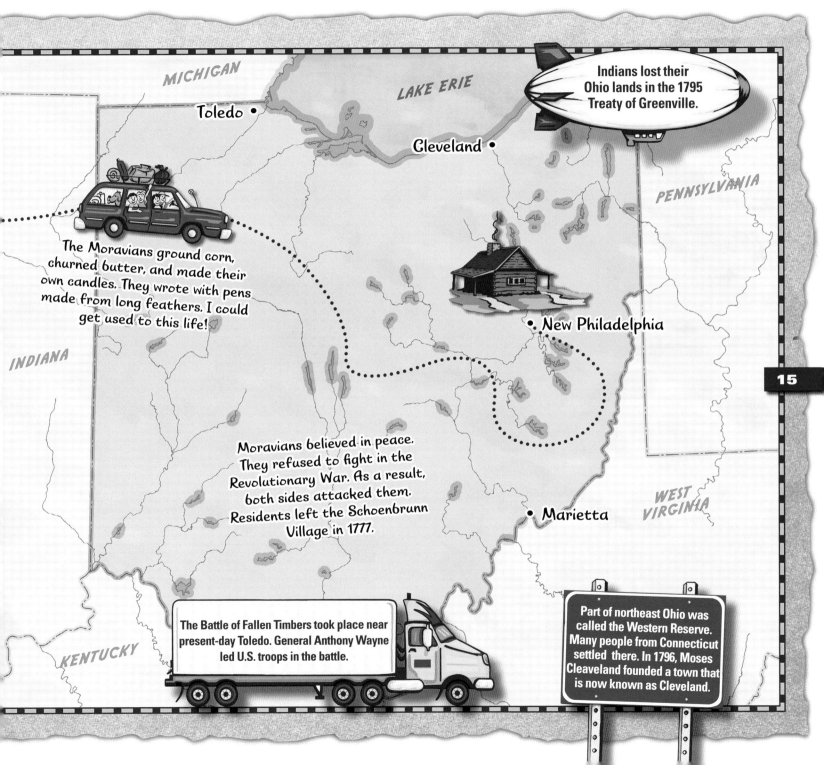

MICHIGAN

LAKE ERIE

Toledo •

Cleveland •

Indians lost their Ohio lands in the 1795 Treaty of Greenville.

PENNSYLVANIA

The Moravians ground corn, churned butter, and made their own candles. They wrote with pens made from long feathers. I could get used to this life!

• New Philadelphia

INDIANA

Moravians believed in peace. They refused to fight in the Revolutionary War. As a result, both sides attacked them. Residents left the Schoenbrunn Village in 1777.

• Marietta

WEST VIRGINIA

The Battle of Fallen Timbers took place near present-day Toledo. General Anthony Wayne led U.S. troops in the battle.

KENTUCKY

Part of northeast Ohio was called the Western Reserve. Many people from Connecticut settled there. In 1796, Moses Cleaveland founded a town that is now known as Cleveland.

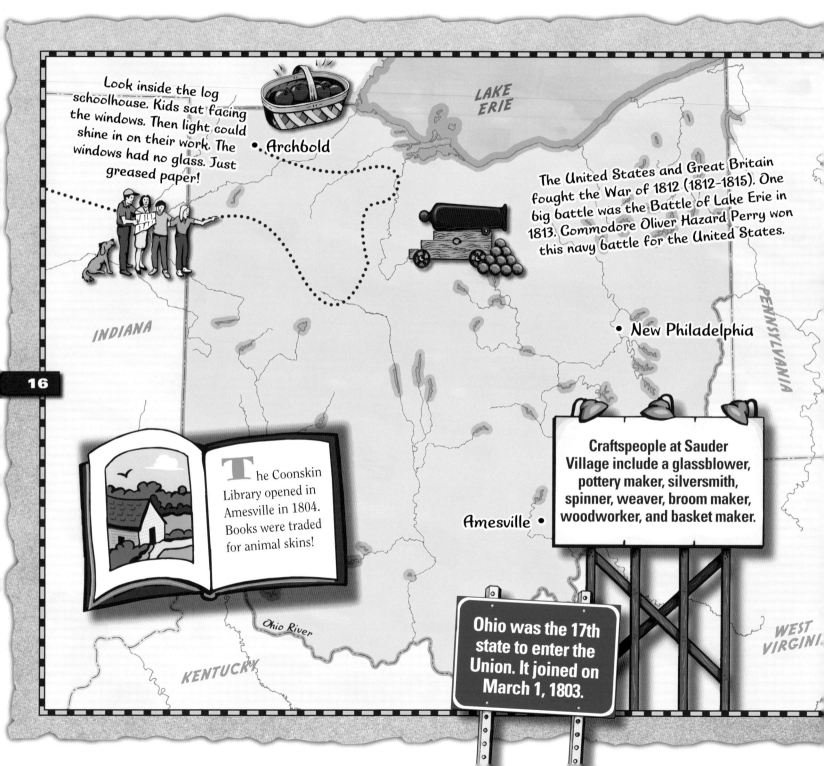

Look inside the log schoolhouse. Kids sat facing the windows. Then light could shine in on their work. The windows had no glass. Just greased paper!

• Archbold

The United States and Great Britain fought the War of 1812 (1812–1815). One big battle was the Battle of Lake Erie in 1813. Commodore Oliver Hazard Perry won this navy battle for the United States.

LAKE ERIE

• New Philadelphia

INDIANA

PENNSYLVANIA

The Coonskin Library opened in Amesville in 1804. Books were traded for animal skins!

Amesville •

Craftspeople at Sauder Village include a glassblower, pottery maker, silversmith, spinner, weaver, broom maker, woodworker, and basket maker.

Ohio River

KENTUCKY

Ohio was the 17th state to enter the Union. It joined on March 1, 1803.

WEST VIRGINI

Historic Sauder Village in Archbold

Learn to milk a cow. Wash clothes on an old scrub board. Chat with the broom maker, blacksmith, and other folks. Need a basket for your apples? Just stop by the basket maker's!

You're visiting Historic Sauder Village. It shows how Ohio **pioneers** lived.

Ohio grew fast in the 1800s. Thousands of settlers poured in. Some started farms by the Ohio River.

Farmers shipped their goods on the river. Those goods then traveled to the Mississippi River. They went south to New Orleans.

Like old-fashioned apple cider? Try some at Sauder Village!

Zoar Village is near New Philadelphia. German people settled there in 1817. They were seeking religious freedom.

Roscoe Village reveals life in an 1830s canal town.

Visit the shopkeepers and craftspeople. Try your hand at dipping candles or making rope. Then climb aboard the **canal** boat. A horse on the bank pulls your boat along!

You're visiting Roscoe Village. It was a canal town in the 1830s. It shows how townspeople along the canals lived.

Ohio built canals to help move goods faster. One canal was the Ohio and Erie Canal. Its north end was at Cleveland, on Lake Erie. Its south end was at Portsmouth, on the Ohio River. The Miami and Erie Canal was another waterway. It ran between Toledo and Cincinnati.

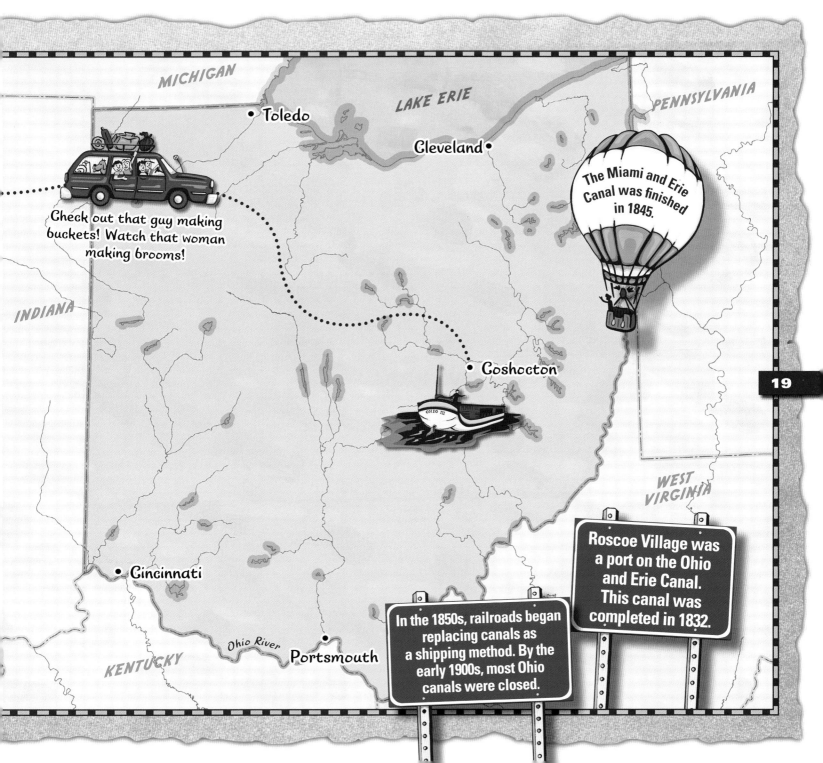

MICHIGAN

LAKE ERIE

PENNSYLVANIA

• Toledo

Cleveland •

Check out that guy making buckets! Watch that woman making brooms!

The Miami and Erie Canal was finished in 1845.

INDIANA

• Coshocton

OHIO III

WEST VIRGINIA

• Cincinnati

Roscoe Village was a port on the Ohio and Erie Canal. This canal was completed in 1832.

In the 1850s, railroads began replacing canals as a shipping method. By the early 1900s, most Ohio canals were closed.

Ohio River

Portsmouth •

KENTUCKY

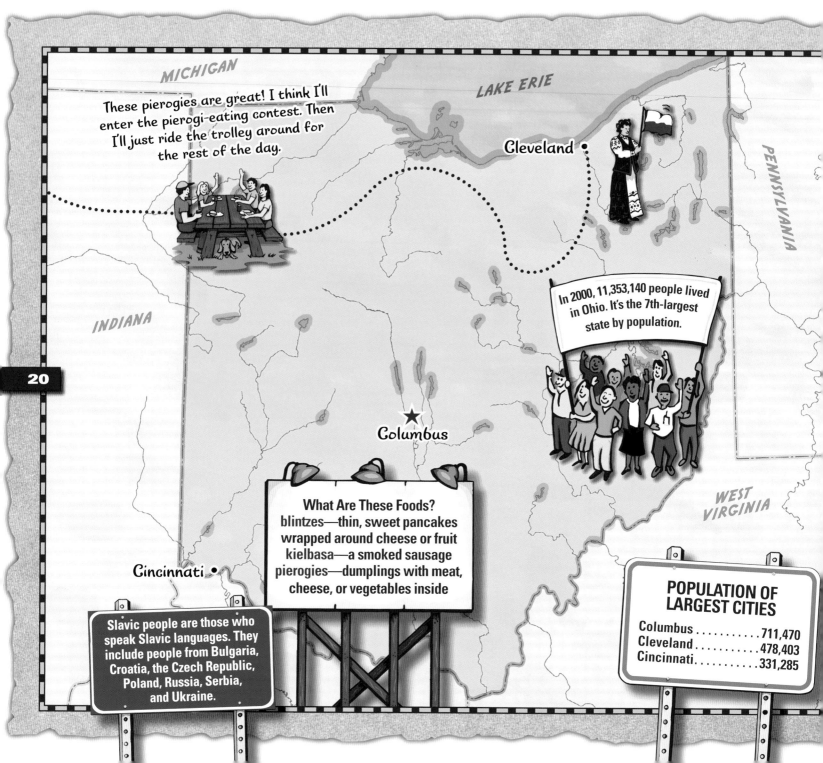

MICHIGAN

LAKE ERIE

PENNSYLVANIA

These pierogies are great! I think I'll enter the pierogi-eating contest. Then I'll just ride the trolley around for the rest of the day.

Cleveland

INDIANA

In 2000, 11,353,140 people lived in Ohio. It's the 7th-largest state by population.

★ Columbus

WEST VIRGINIA

What Are These Foods?
blintzes—thin, sweet pancakes wrapped around cheese or fruit
kielbasa—a smoked sausage
pierogies—dumplings with meat, cheese, or vegetables inside

Cincinnati

Slavic people are those who speak Slavic languages. They include people from Bulgaria, Croatia, the Czech Republic, Poland, Russia, Serbia, and Ukraine.

POPULATION OF LARGEST CITIES
Columbus 711,470
Cleveland 478,403
Cincinnati. 331,285

Cleveland's Slavic Village Harvest Festival

Snarf down some pierogies. Chomp on a kielbasa or two. Then for dessert, try those yummy blintzes. You're at the Slavic Village Harvest Festival! It's held in Cleveland's Warszawa neighborhood. That's one of the nation's largest Polish American communities.

Many **immigrants** settled in Ohio. Cleveland's **industries** made it an attractive new home. Now the city has dozens of **ethnic** neighborhoods. Some were settled by Polish or Hungarian immigrants. Puerto Ricans and Italians built communities there, too. So did people from Asia and the Middle East.

Yum! Want to try some tasty kielbasa? Head to the Slavic Village Harvest Festival!

21

Check out this wheel from the early 1900s! It's on display at Goodyear World of Rubber.

John D. Rockefeller opened the Standard Oil Company of Ohio in 1870.

Goodyear World of Rubber in Akron

Akron is famous for making rubber tires. Just visit Goodyear World of Rubber. You'll see a lot more than car tires! You'll see moon buggy tires and an artificial heart. Both are made with Akron rubber.

Many new industries developed in the mid-1800s. Ohio factories made foods, clothing, and farm tools. Cincinnati became a center for steelmaking.

Charles Goodyear found a way to make rubber strong. In 1870, Benjamin Goodrich opened Akron's first rubber factory. Akron's Goodyear Tire and Rubber Company opened later. Soon, new machines called automobiles became popular. Then Akron made millions of tires!

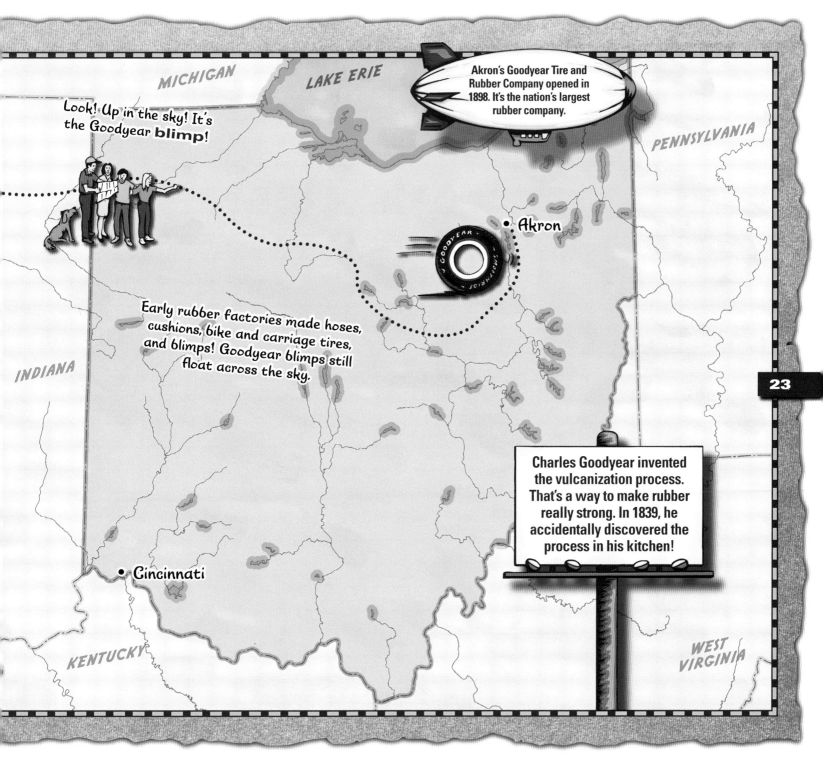

Look! Up in the sky! It's the Goodyear **blimp**!

Akron's Goodyear Tire and Rubber Company opened in 1898. It's the nation's largest rubber company.

• Akron

Early rubber factories made hoses, cushions, bike and carriage tires, and blimps! Goodyear blimps still float across the sky.

• Cincinnati

Charles Goodyear invented the vulcanization process. That's a way to make rubber really strong. In 1839, he accidentally discovered the process in his kitchen!

MICHIGAN

LAKE ERIE

PENNSYLVANIA

INDIANA

KENTUCKY

WEST VIRGINIA

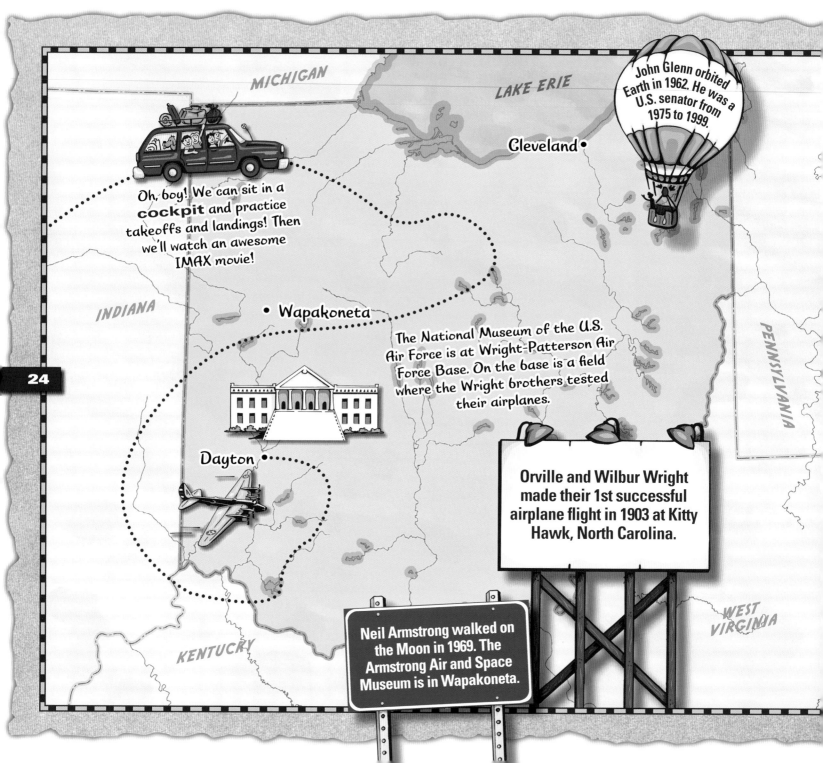

MICHIGAN

LAKE ERIE

John Glenn orbited Earth in 1962. He was a U.S. senator from 1975 to 1999.

Cleveland •

Oh, boy! We can sit in a **cockpit** and practice takeoffs and landings! Then we'll watch an awesome IMAX movie!

INDIANA

• Wapakoneta

The National Museum of the U.S. Air Force is at Wright-Patterson Air Force Base. On the base is a field where the Wright brothers tested their airplanes.

Dayton •

PENNSYLVANIA

Orville and Wilbur Wright made their 1st successful airplane flight in 1903 at Kitty Hawk, North Carolina.

WEST VIRGINIA

KENTUCKY

Neil Armstrong walked on the Moon in 1969. The Armstrong Air and Space Museum is in Wapakoneta.

Dayton's Air Force Museum

Do you like Snoopy in the *Peanuts* cartoons? Sometimes Snoopy flies an airplane. It's an early plane called a Sopwith Camel. You'll see a real Sopwith Camel in Dayton. It's at the National Museum of the U.S. Air Force. You'll see dozens of military airplanes there.

Ohio is proud of its flight history. The Wright brothers lived and worked in Dayton. They invented the first airplane. Astronaut Neil Armstrong was born in Ohio. He was the first person to walk on the Moon. Ohioan John Glenn was another astronaut. He was the first U.S. astronaut to **orbit** Earth.

Prepare for takeoff! Or just head to the National Museum of the U.S. Air Force.

The John H. Glenn Research Center is in Cleveland. This center develops engines for aircraft and spacecraft.

Vroom! Technicians put together motorcycles in Marysville.

Honda's Marysville auto plant was the 1st Japanese auto plant in the United States.

Touring the Honda Motorcycle Factory in Marysville

Do you like motorcycles? Then you'll love Honda's motorcycle factory. Everything's arranged in long lines. Each worker along a line has one job. Some workers add tiny engine parts. Others add brakes or handlebars. At the end, out come shiny motorbikes. *Vroom*!

Manufacturing is a huge industry in Ohio. The top factory goods are transportation equipment. That includes cars and trucks. And don't forget all those motorcycles! Chemicals are another important factory product. Those include paint and cleaning products. Ohio also makes foods. Some food plants pack meat. Others make soup, frozen dinners, or pizzas!

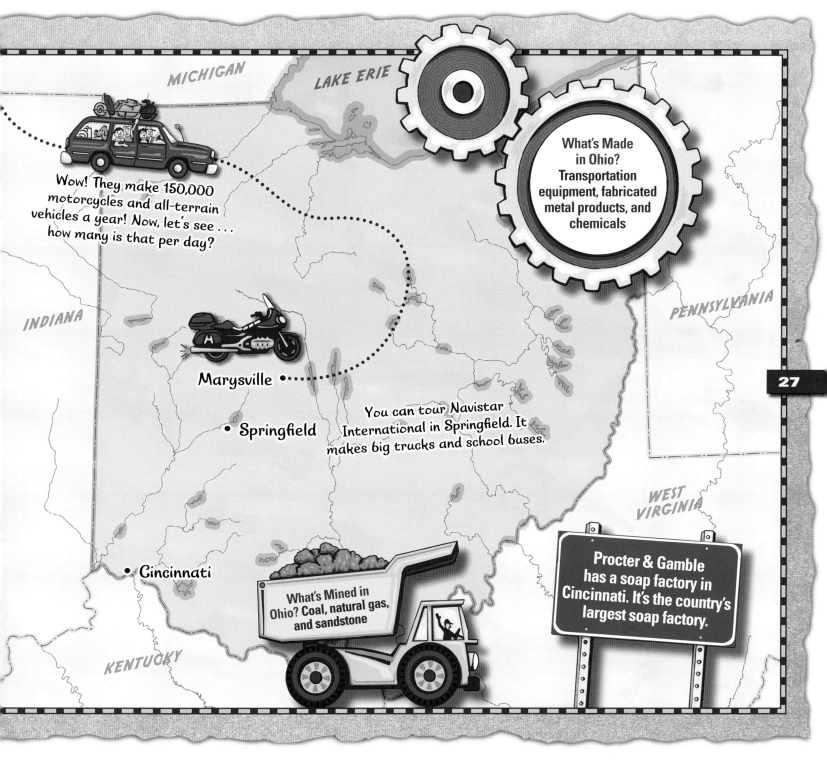

MICHIGAN

LAKE ERIE

Wow! They make 150,000 motorcycles and all-terrain vehicles a year! Now, let's see . . . how many is that per day?

What's Made in Ohio? Transportation equipment, fabricated metal products, and chemicals

PENNSYLVANIA

INDIANA

Marysville

Springfield

You can tour Navistar International in Springfield. It makes big trucks and school buses.

WEST VIRGINIA

Cincinnati

What's Mined in Ohio? Coal, natural gas, and sandstone

Procter & Gamble has a soap factory in Cincinnati. It's the country's largest soap factory.

KENTUCKY

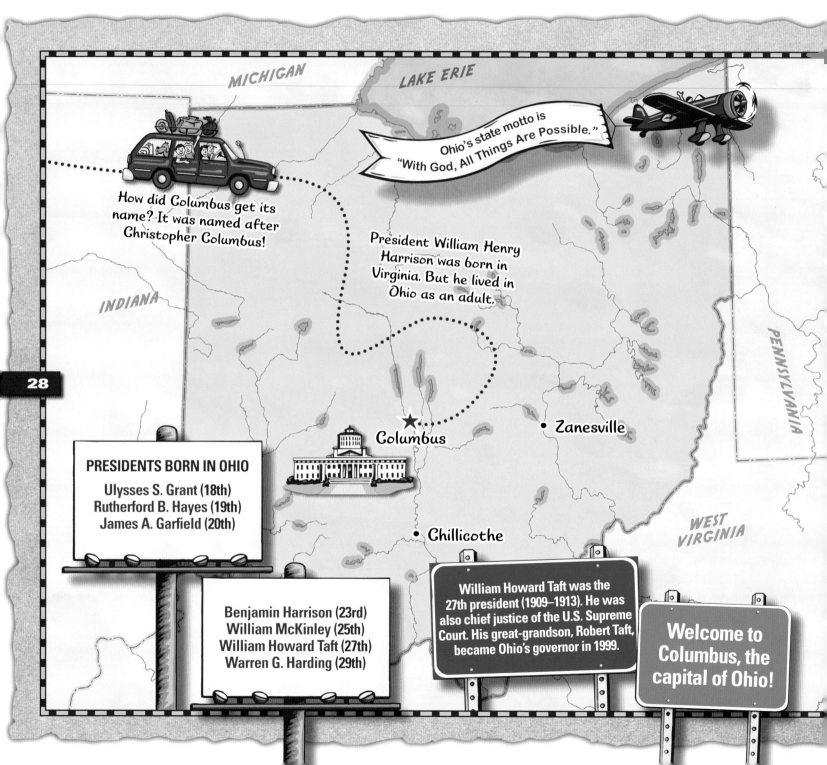

MICHIGAN

LAKE ERIE

INDIANA

PENNSYLVANIA

WEST VIRGINIA

How did Columbus get its name? It was named after Christopher Columbus!

Ohio's state motto is "With God, All Things Are Possible."

President William Henry Harrison was born in Virginia. But he lived in Ohio as an adult.

★ Columbus

• Zanesville

• Chillicothe

PRESIDENTS BORN IN OHIO

Ulysses S. Grant (18th)
Rutherford B. Hayes (19th)
James A. Garfield (20th)

Benjamin Harrison (23rd)
William McKinley (25th)
William Howard Taft (27th)
Warren G. Harding (29th)

William Howard Taft was the 27th president (1909–1913). He was also chief justice of the U.S. Supreme Court. His great-grandson, Robert Taft, became Ohio's governor in 1999.

Welcome to Columbus, the capital of Ohio!

The State Capitol in Columbus

Walk inside the massive state capitol. Then look up. High overhead is a design in stained glass. It's the state seal. It shows a golden sun rising over mountains. A river flows beneath the mountains. There's a field and bundles of wheat and arrows. It's great to see this on a sunny day. The colors are dazzling!

The capitol houses many state government offices. Ohio's government has three branches. The governor heads one branch. This branch sees that laws are carried out. Another branch makes laws for the state. Judges make up the third branch. They listen to cases in courts. They decide whether someone has broken the law.

Ohio lawmakers are hard at work inside the capitol.

Columbus became Ohio's capital in 1816. Chillicothe and Zanesville were the capitals before that.

Look, no hands! Check out the high-wire cycle at COSI.

Watch a team of rats play basketball. Learn how race cars can go so fast. Feel electricity surging through your body. It makes your hair stand straight out!

You're exploring Toledo's Center of Science and Industry. It's called COSI for short. At COSI, you don't just look at stuff. You really get involved! You try out science ideas yourself. Then you see how science laws work.

You'll learn about weather and electricity. You'll explore your own body and mind. And you'll discover the science secrets behind sports. Think about those rats throwing basketballs through a hoop. They must have a secret!

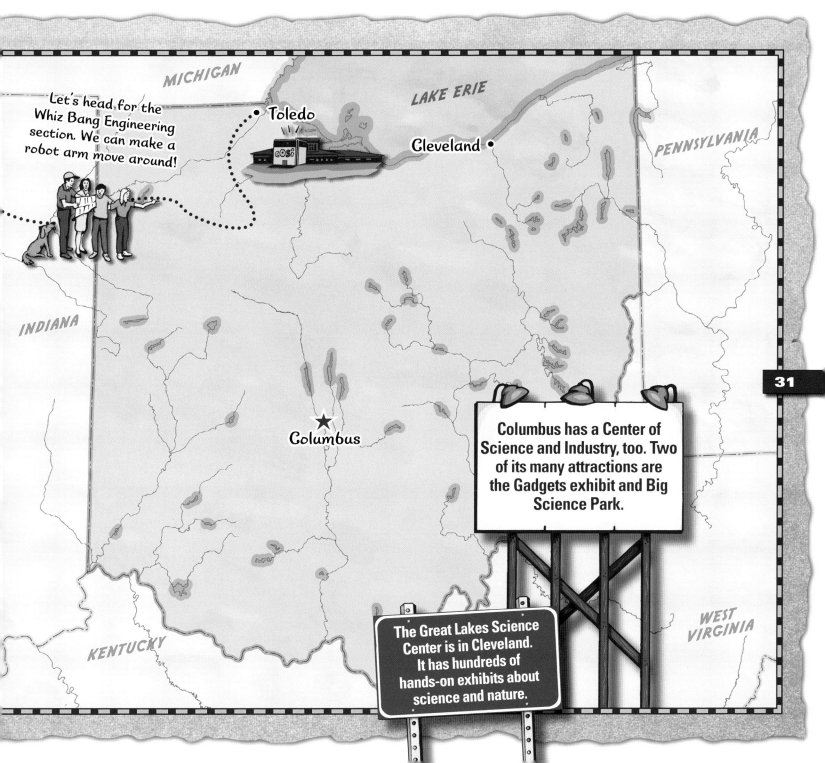

Let's head for the Whiz Bang Engineering section. We can make a robot arm move around!

MICHIGAN

LAKE ERIE

Toledo

Cleveland

PENNSYLVANIA

INDIANA

★ Columbus

Columbus has a Center of Science and Industry, too. Two of its many attractions are the Gadgets exhibit and Big Science Park.

The Great Lakes Science Center is in Cleveland. It has hundreds of hands-on exhibits about science and nature.

WEST VIRGINIA

KENTUCKY

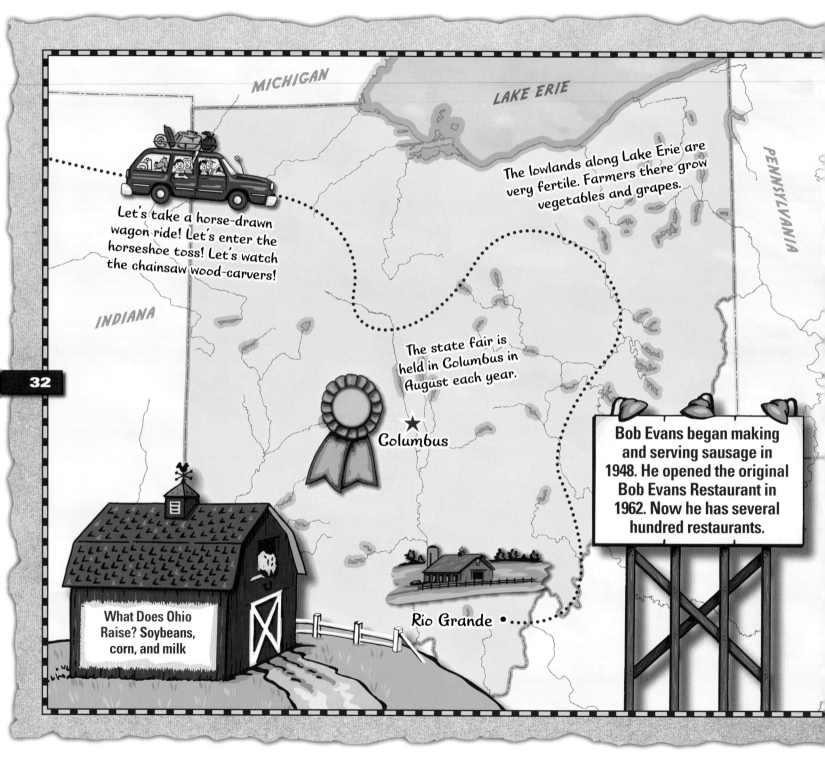

The Bob Evans Farm Festival in Rio Grande

Pet the farm animals. See the sheep get their wool cut off. Watch dressed-up tractors do square dances. Then enter the hog-calling contest. It's the Bob Evans Farm Festival!

This is one of Ohio's many farm celebrations. Farmers in Ohio are pretty busy. Farmland covers about half the state. Soybeans and corn are the top farm products. Ohio is a leader in growing both crops.

Ohio's dairy farmers raise cows for their milk. Many farmers raise beef cattle, hogs, and sheep. Bob Evans raised hogs on his farm. He turned them into delicious sausage!

A craftswoman designs scarecrows. Her work is featured at the Bob Evans Farm Festival.

Johnny Appleseed (1774–1845) was a pioneer hero. He wandered through Ohio planting apple trees. His real name was John Chapman.

These girls sure do look alike! Twins gather every year in Twinsburg.

Twinsburg held its 1st Twins Days festival in 1976. Only 37 sets of twins were there.

34

Are you seeing double? No. You've just wandered into the Twins Days festival! It's the world's largest gathering of twins. And it happens in Twinsburg!

About 3,000 sets of twins attend every year. They march in the Double Take Parade. They take part in the Twins' Talent Show. And they enter some fun contests.

Triplets and quadruplets are welcome, too. What about people who were not multiple-birth babies? Can they attend? Of course. They just pay more to get in!

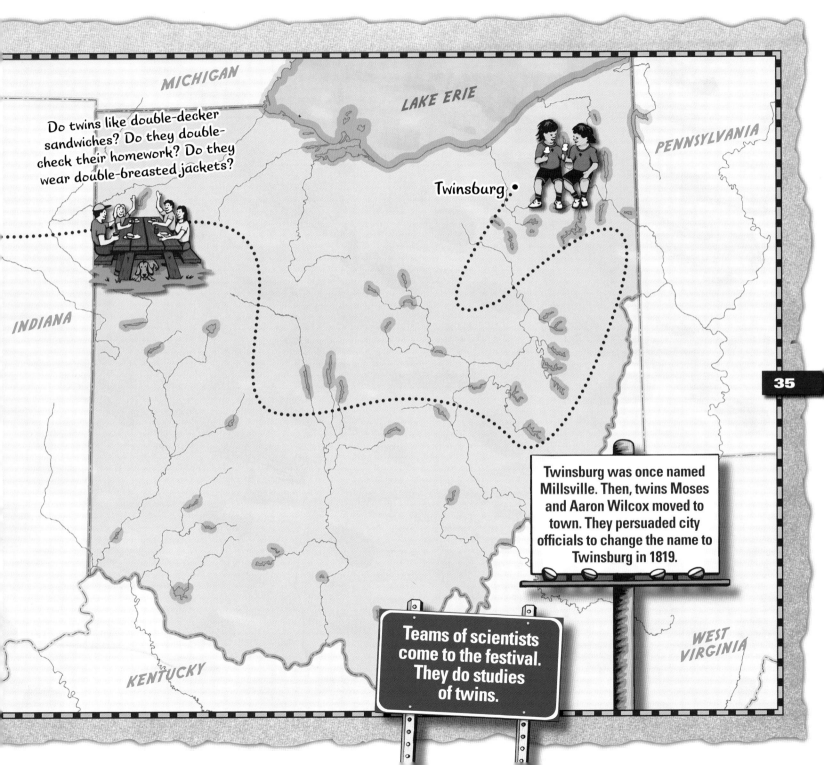

Do twins like double-decker sandwiches? Do they double-check their homework? Do they wear double-breasted jackets?

Twinsburg

Twinsburg was once named Millsville. Then, twins Moses and Aaron Wilcox moved to town. They persuaded city officials to change the name to Twinsburg in 1819.

Teams of scientists come to the festival. They do studies of twins.

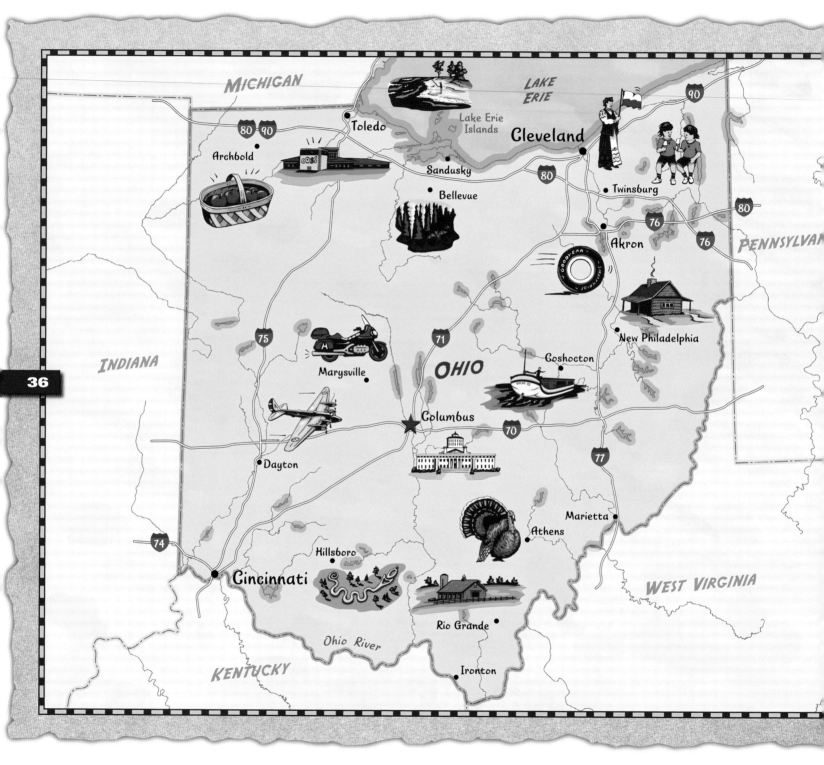

OUR TRIP

We visited many amazing places on our trip! We also met a lot of interesting people along the way. Look at the map on the left. Use your finger to trace all the places we have been.

What is the name of Ohio's largest cave? See page 7 for the answer.

Who founded Cleveland? Page 15 has the answer.

What year did Ohio enter the Union? See page 16 for the answer.

What is the population of Cincinnati? Look on page 20 for the answer.

Where is the Armstrong Air and Space Museum located? Page 24 has the answer.

What is the country's largest soap factory? Turn to page 27 for the answer.

When did the original Bob Evans Restaurant open? Look on page 32 and find out!

What was Johnny Appleseed's real name? Turn to page 33 for the answer.

That was a great trip! We have traveled all over Ohio! There are a few places that we didn't have time for, though. Next time, we plan to visit Cedar Point in Sandusky. We can ride the roller coasters and swim at Soak City! The amusement park also features live shows and a miniature golf course.

More Places to Visit in Ohio

WORDS TO KNOW

blimp (BLIMP) a gas-filled aircraft with no wings

canal (kuh-NAL) a long, narrow waterway dug by humans

caverns (KAV-ernz) caves

cockpit (KOK-pit) the part of an aircraft where the pilot sits

colonists (KOL-uh-nists) people who settle a new land for their home country

earthworks (URTH-wurks) large structures built out of soil

ethnic (ETH-nik) relating to a person's race or nationality

glaciers (GLAY-shurz) sheets of ice that move like flowing rivers

immigrants (IM-uh-gruhnts) people who leave their home country and move to another country

industries (IN-duh-streez) types of business

missionaries (MISH-uh-ner-eez) people who move somewhere to spread their religion

orbit (OR-bit) to travel in a circular pattern around an object

pioneers (pye-uh-NEERZ) people who move into an unsettled land

prehistoric (pree-hi-STOR-ik) taking place before people began writing down their history

Ohio covers 40,948 square miles (106,056 sq km). It's the 35th-largest state in size.

STATE SYMBOLS

State animal: White-tailed deer

State beverage: Tomato juice

State bird: Cardinal

State flower: Scarlet carnation

State fossil: *Isotelus* (trilobite)

State gemstone: Ohio flint

State insect: Ladybug

State poetry day: Third Friday in October

State reptile: Black racer (snake)

State rock song: "Hang On Sloopy" by Rick Derringer

State tree: Ohio buckeye

State wildflower: Large white trillium

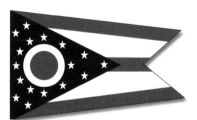

State flag

State seal

STATE SONG

"Beautiful Ohio"

Words by Wilbert McBride (earlier, original words by Ballard MacDonald),
music by Mary Earl

I sailed away;
Wandered afar;
Crossed the mighty restless sea;
Looked for where I ought to be.
Cities so grand, mountains above,
Led to this land I love.

Chorus:
Beautiful Ohio, where the golden grain
Dwarf the lovely flowers in the summer rain.
Cities rising high, silhouette the sky.
Freedom is supreme in this majestic land;
Mighty factories seem to hum a tune, so grand.
Beautiful Ohio, thy wonders are in view,
Land where my dreams all come true!

FAMOUS PEOPLE

Armstrong, Neil (1930–), astronaut, the 1st man to walk on the Moon

Cartwright, Nancy (1959–), the voice of Bart Simpson

Creech, Sharon (1945–), children's author

Custer, George Armstrong (1839–1876), army general

Dandridge, Dorothy (1922–1965), actor

Edison, Thomas Alva (1847–1931), inventor

Gable, Clark (1901–1960), actor

Garfield, James (1831–1881), 20th U.S. president

Gish, Lillian (1893–1993), actor

Grant, Ulysses S. (1822–1885), 18th U.S. president

Hamilton, Virginia (1936–2002), children's author

Hayes, Rutherford B. (1822–1893), 19th U.S. president

Lin, Maya (1959–), artist

Martin, Dean (1917–1995), entertainer

Morrison, Toni (1931–), author

Newman, Paul (1925–), actor

Oakley, Annie (1860–1926), markswoman

Spielberg, Steven (1946–), film director

Tecumseh (1768–1813), American Indian chief

Wright, Wilbur (1867-1912), Orville (1871-1948), aviation pioneers

Young, Cy (1867–1955), baseball player

TO FIND OUT MORE

At the Library

Boekhoff, P. M., and Stuart A. Kallen. *Ohio.* San Diego: Kidhaven Press, 2002.

McLeese, Don. *Tecumseh.* Vero Beach, Fla.: Rourke Publishing, 2004.

Rappaport, Doreen, and Bryan Collier (illustrator). *Freedom River.* New York: Jump at the Sun/Hyperion Books for Children, 2000.

Schonberg, Marcia, and Bruce Langton (illustrator). *B Is for Buckeye: An Ohio Alphabet.* Chelsea, Mich.: Sleeping Bear Press, 2000.

Zemlicka, Shannon. *Neil Armstrong.* Minneapolis: Lerner, 2003.

On the Web

Visit our home page for lots of links about Ohio:
http://www.childsworld.com/links

Note to Parents, Teachers, and Librarians: We routinely verify our Web links to make sure they are safe, active sites—so encourage your readers to check them out!

Places to Visit or Contact

Ohio Division of Travel and Tourism
PO Box 1001
Columbus, OH 43216-1001
800/282-5393
For more information about traveling in Ohio

The Ohio Historical Society
1982 Velma Avenue
Columbus, OH 43211
614/297-2300
For more information about the history of Ohio

INDEX

Bye, Buckeye State. We had a great time. We'll come back soon!